Orchestra Accompaniment *series*

T0040941

3 Famous Tenor Arias

On the cover: John Singer Sargent, American, 1856-1925, *Rehearsal of the Pas de Loup Orchestra at the Cirque d'Hiver*, oil on canvas, 1878, 36 $^5/_8$" x 28 $^3/_4$", Anonymous loan, 81.1972. Copyright © 1996, The Art Institute of Chicago, All Rights Reserved.

ISBN 978-0-7935-6892-5

HAL•LEONARD® CORPORATION
7777 W. BLUEMOUND RD. P.O. BOX 13819 MILWAUKEE, WI 53213

Orchestra Accompaniment
series

3 Famous Tenor Arias

ON THE RECORDING

John Oakman, tenor
Czech Symphony Orchestra conducted by Julian Bigg

with the Prague Philharmonic Choir
Christopher Todd Landor, producer
Eric Tomlinson; Daniel Gable, engineers
recorded at the FHS studios, Prague, 6/92

Contents

RIGOLETTO
La donna è mobile

Giuseppe Verdi's Rigoletto, with text by Francesco Maria Piave, is based on the play *Le Roi s'amuse* (The King Amuses Himself) by Victor Hugo. Composed in forty days during 1851, the opera was premiered at the Teatro la Fenice, Venice on March 11, 1851.

Rigoletto, the hunchback, is the court jester of the amoral Duke of Mantua, in the sixteenth-century. When the elderly Count Monterone finds his daughter seduced by the Duke, Rigoletto mimics him in his role as jester. The Count places a father's curse on Rigoletto. The Duke's underlings discover that Rigoletto has beautiful young daughter hidden away in seclusion. Assuming she is his mistress, they trick Rigoletto into helping them abduct her to be delivered to the Duke. She is actually Gilda, Rigoletto's own daughter. The Duke has been visiting Gilda, in disguise, for some time. Gilda loves him. Enraged, Rigoletto hires an assassin, Sparafucile, to kill the Duke. In Act III Sparafucile's sister, Maddalena, lures the Duke to a lonely inn. He disguises himself as a soldier. The Duke drinks wine as he sings "La donna è mobile" about the inconstancy of women, but reveals more of his own inconstancy than anything else. (Maddalena is taken with the Duke, and persuades Sparafucile to kill a stranger instead to supply Rigoletto with a dead body. The "stranger" at the door turns out to be Gilda in disguise, who dies in Rigoletto's arms.)

La donna è mobile	*Woman is flighty*
qual piuma al vento;	*like a feather in a breeze;*
muta d'accento	*inconsistent in word*
e di pensiero.	*and in thought.*
Sempre un amabile	*An adorable*
leggiadro viso,	*pretty face,*
in pianto o in riso,	*weeping or laughing,*
è menzognero.	*is always deceitful.*
E sempre misero	*Eternally miserable*
che a lei s'affida,	*is he who confides in her,*
chi le confida	*who rashly entrusts*
mal cauto il core!	*his heart to her!*
Pur mai non sentesi	*But he who never tastes*
felice appieno	*love upon that breast*
chi su quel seno	*will never know*
non liba amore!	*complete happiness.*

LA BOHÈME
Che gelida manina

La bohème was first performed at Turin on February 1, 1896. Since that time it has remained one of the world's most familiar and most often produced operas. The libretto, by Giuseppe Giacosa and Luigi Illica, is based on the French novel by Henry Murger, *Scenes de la Vie de Bohème*. The opera takes place in the Latin quarter of Paris, c. 1830. (Productions have played in it many time periods, the most common being the 1890s, the time of the opera's premiere.)

La bohème is the tale of a group of "Bohemians" living in a garret in Paris. Rodolfo (a poet), Marcello (a painter), Colline (a philosopher), and Schaunard (a musician) make up the band of friends. Act I takes place on Christmas Eve in the chilly garret apartment. Marcello, Schaunard and Colline leave to celebrate the holiday out in a café, but Rodolfo stays behind to work on a newspaper piece that is due. There is a knock at the door. A pretty, young woman who lives in the same building asks if he can light her candle, which has blown out in the dark stairway. She comes in, and for some reason Rodolfo's candle also blows out. (He might have helped that to happen.) Mimì drops her key, and together, on their knees they look for it. Suddenly, Rodolfo's hand touches hers. Romance has been in the air since she first appeared in the doorway, and the poet Rodolfo gives voice to his feelings in "Che gelida manina."

Che gelida manina—	*What an icy hand—*
se la lasci riscaldar.	*let it be warmed.*
Cercar che giova?	*What help is searching?*
Al buio non si trova.	*In darkness it won't be found.*
Ma per fortuna è una notte di luna,	*But by luck it is a moonlit night,*
e qui la luna l'abbiamo vicina.	*and here the moon is nearby.*
Aspetti, signorina—	*Wait, miss—*
le dirò con due parole	*I'll tell you in a few words*
chi son, e che faccio, come vivo.	*who I am, what I do, how I live.*
Vuole?	*Would that please you?*
Chi son? Sono un poeta.	*Who am I? I am a poet.*
Che cosa faccio? Scrivo.	*What do I do? Write.*
E come vivo? Vivo.	*How do I live? Alive.*
In povertà mia lieta	*In poverty I am happy*
scialo da gran signore	*I squander like a great man*
rime ed inni d'amore.	*rhymes and anthems of love.*
Per sogni e per chimere	*In fantasies and daydreams*
e per castelli in aria,	*and castles in the air;*
l'anima ho milionaria.	*my soul is a millionaire.*
Talor dal mio forziere	*Sometimes from my coffers*
ruban tutti i gioielli due	*all jewels are stolen by two*
ladri: gli occhi belli.	*thieves: beautiful eyes.*
V'entrar con voi pur ora,	*They entered with you now,*
ed i miei sogni usati	*and my worn dreams*
e i bei sogni miei	*and my sweet dreams*
tosto si dileguar!	*promptly vanished!*
Ma il furto non m'accora	*But the burglary does not sadden me*
poichè v'ha preso stanza	*since in its place is*
la dolce speranza!	*sweet hope!*
Or che mi conoscete	*Now that you know me*
parlate voi.	*you speak.*
Deh! parlate.	*Oh! speak.*
Chi siete?	*Who are you?*
Vi piaccia dir!	*Will you please speak?*

TURANDOT
Nessun dorma!

Turandot was Giacomo Puccini's last work, and was left unfinished at the composer's death in 1924. The libretto, by Giuseppe Adami and Renato Simoni, is based on a Carlo Gozzi drama of the same name. His friend Franco Alfano consulted the composer's notes and outlines to complete the score, which has always been the standard edition of the opera that is performed. But at the opera's premiere on April 25, 1926, to honor Puccini, conductor Arturo Toscanini stopped the premiere performance halfway through the third act, turned to the audience and said, "Here is where the Maestro put down his pen."

Turandot is the icy and mysterious princess of Peking who decrees that she will marry the first man who can answer three riddles. Those who fail will be killed. The Unknown Prince (Calaf) arrives, is reunited with his father (Timur) and loyal slave-girl (Liù), and is determined to take on the challenge of the riddles. The Prince guesses the riddles correctly. Princess Turandot is shocked and anxious, and pleads with the Emperor to release her from the agreement to marry. The Unknown Prince intervenes, offering a riddle of his own to her. She has one day to find out his name. If she does, he will still die. If she does not, she will marry him. The royal court sends out orders throughout the city that no one may sleep ("Nessun dorma"), upon penalty of death, until the name is discovered. Hearing the guards and the people saying the proclamation, Calaf echoes the phrase himself as he begins his aria, sung at night. He is confident of his victory in the new day.

Nessun dorma!	*No one sleeps!*
Tu pure, o Principessa,	*You too, oh Princess,*
nella tua fredda stanza	*in your chilly chamber*
guardi le stelle	*are looking at the stars*
che tremano d'amore	*which twinkle with love*
e di speranza!	*and hope!*
Ma il mio mistero è chiuso in me,	*But my mystery is hidden in me,*
il nome mio nessun saprà!	*my name that no one will know!*
No, no, sulla tua bocca lo dirò,	*No, no, only on your lips will I say it*
quando la luce splenderà!	*when the light shines!*
Ed il mio bacio scioglierà il silenzio	*And my kiss will break the silence*
che ti fa mia!	*that makes you mine*
[chorus:	
Il nome suo nessun saprà	*[His name no one will know*
E noi dovrem ahimè, morir!]	*and alas, we will have to die!]*
Dilegua, o notte!	*Vanish, oh night;*
tramontate stelle!	*let the stars fade!*
All'alba vincerò!	*At daybreak, victory!*

The Arias

Che gelinda manina
from LA BOHÈME

Giacomo Puccini
1896

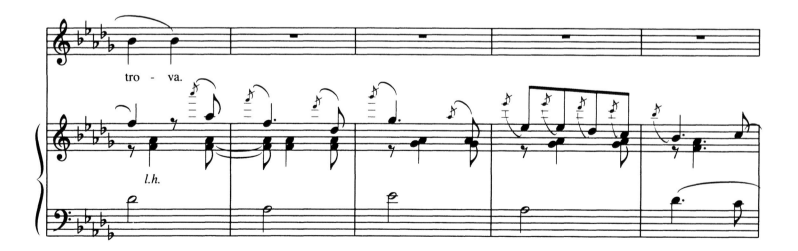

Ma per for-tu-naèu-na not - te di lu - na,_____ e qui la

lu - na l'ab-bia-mo vi-ci-na. A - spet-ti, si-gno-ri-na le di-

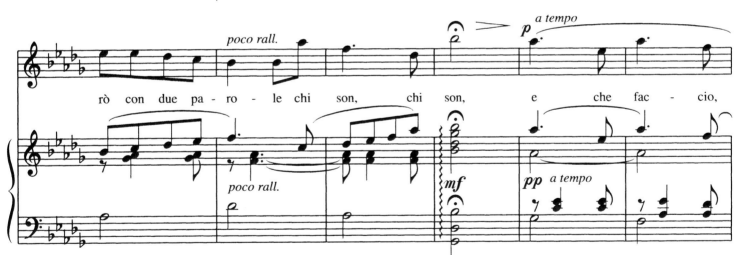

rò con due pa-ro - le chi son, chi son, e che fac - cio,

co - me vi - vo. Vuo - le? Chi

Andante sostenuto

son?— Chi son? So-no un po - e - ta. Che co-sa fac - cio?

Scri - vo. E co-me vi - vo? Vi-vo.

Andante lento ♩ 52

In po - ver-tà mia lie - ta scia-lo da gran si-

gno - re———————ri - me ed in - ni d'a - mo - re. Per so - gni e per chi-

me - re e per ca-stel-li in a - ria,_____ l'a-ni-ma ho mi - lio - na -

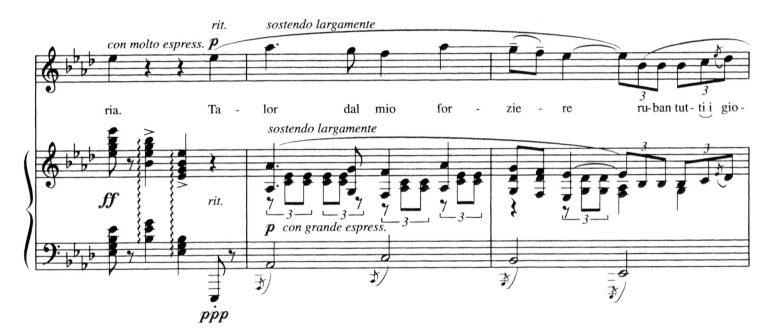

ria. Ta - lor dal mio for - zie - re ru-ban tut - ti i gio -

iel - li due la-dri: gli oc - chi bel - li. V'en-trar con voi pur o - ra,

ed i miei so - gni u - sa - ti e i bei so - gni mie - i

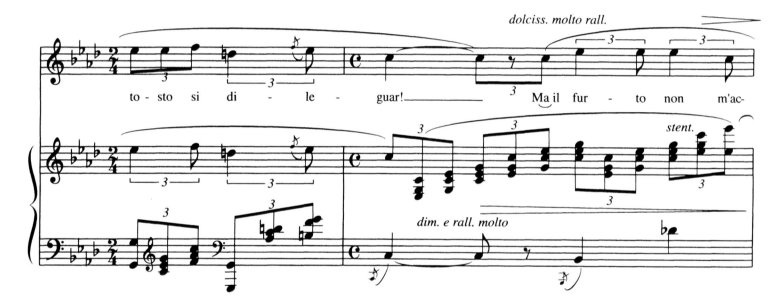

to - sto si di - le - guar! Ma il fur - to non m'ac-

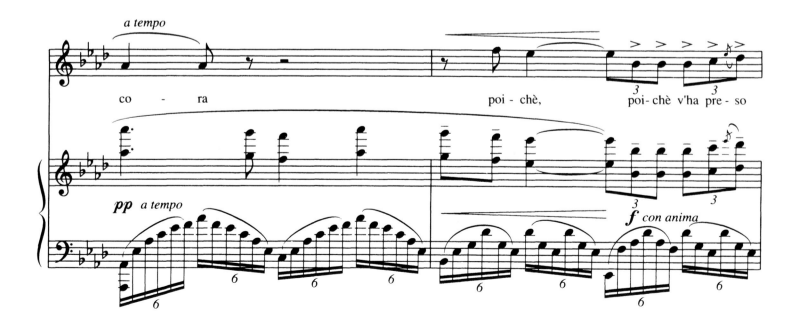

co - ra poi - chè, poi - chè v'ha pre - so

La donna è mobile
from RIGOLETTO

Giuseppe Verdi
1851

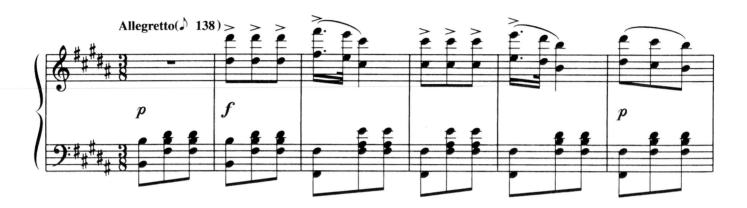

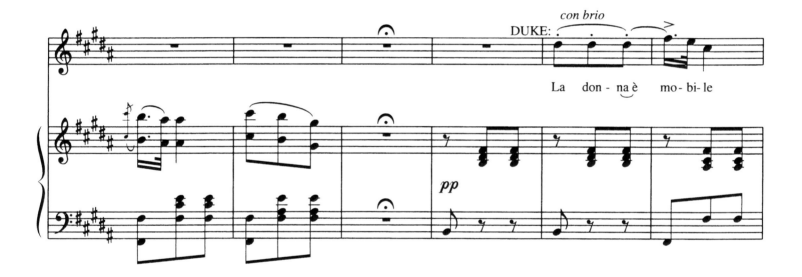

La don-na è mo-bi-le

qual piu- ma al ven - to; mu - ta d'ac - cen - to e di pen-

sie - ro.   Sem - pre un a - ma - bi - le   leg - gia - dro   vi - so,

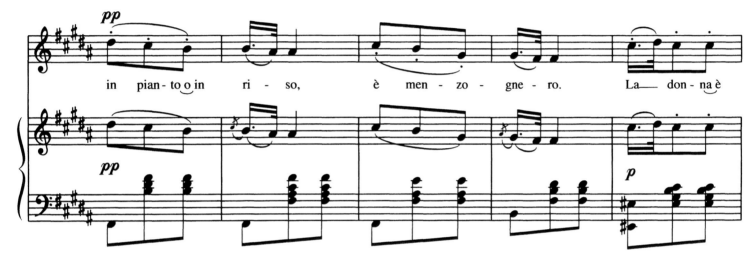

in pian - to o in   ri - so,   è men - zo - gne - ro.   La__ don - na è

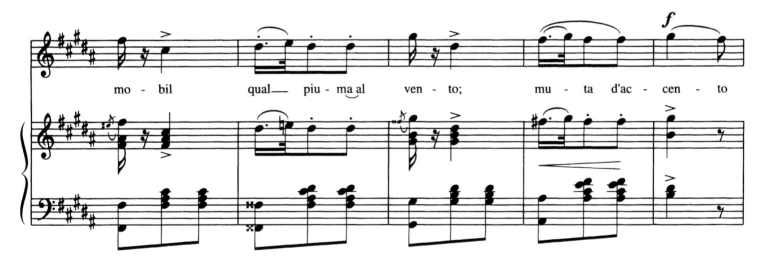

mo - bil   qual__ piu - ma al ven - to;   mu - ta d'ac - cen - to

e__ di pen - sier,

e___ di pen - sier,   e,_____

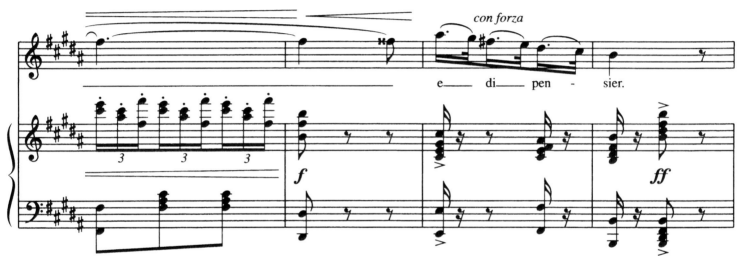

con forza

e___ di pen - sier.

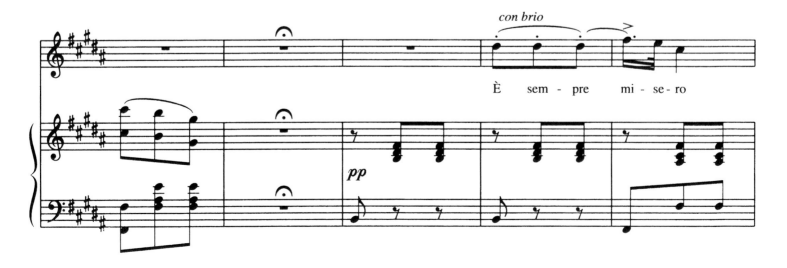

con brio

È sem - pre mi - se - ro

chi a lei s'af - fi - da, chi le con - fi - da mal cau - to il

co - re! Pur mai non sen - te - si fe - li - ce ap - pie - no

chi su quel se - no non li - ba a - mo - re! La___ don - na è

mo - bil qual___ piu - ma al ven - to; mu - ta d'ac - cen - to

e___ di pen - sier,

e___ 3 di pen - sier, e,___

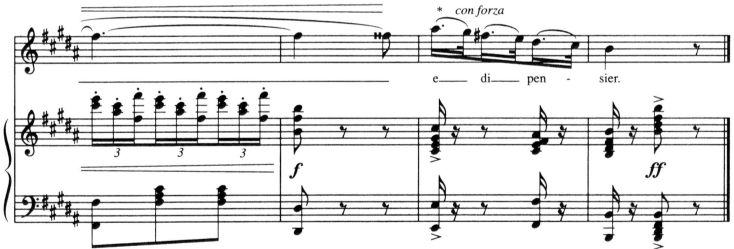

con forza

e___ di pen - sier.

*This cadenza has become traditional; begin the held F♯ two measures later than written.

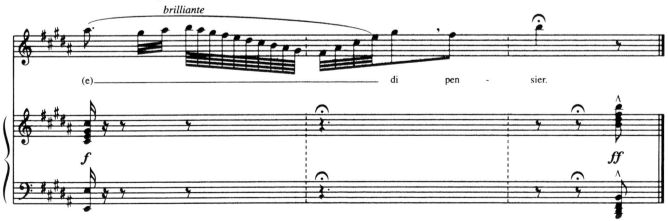

brilliante

(e)_____ di pen - sier.

Nessun dorma!
from TURANDOT

Giacomo Puccini
1926

ran - za! ____ Ma il mio mi - ste - ro è chiu - so in me,

il no - me mio nes - sun sa - prà! No, no, sul - la tua boc - ca lo di -

rò, _____ quan - do la lu - ce splen - de - rà! ____

Ed il mio ba - cio scio - glie - rà il si - len - zio ____ che ti fa

WOMEN'S CHORUS:

mi - a!   Il no - me suo nes - sun sa -

prà. _____ E noi do - vrem ahi - mè, mo -

THE PRINCE:
con anima

Di - le - gua, o not - te! tra - mon - ta - te,

rir, mo - rir!

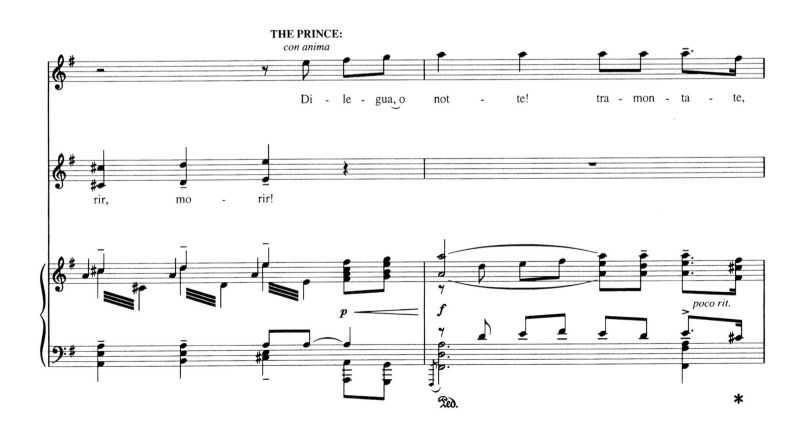

poco rit.

poco rit.

stel - le! Tra - mon - ta - te, stel - le! Al - l'al - ba vin - ce -

cresc. *poco allarg.*

rò! Vin - ce - rò! Vin - ce -

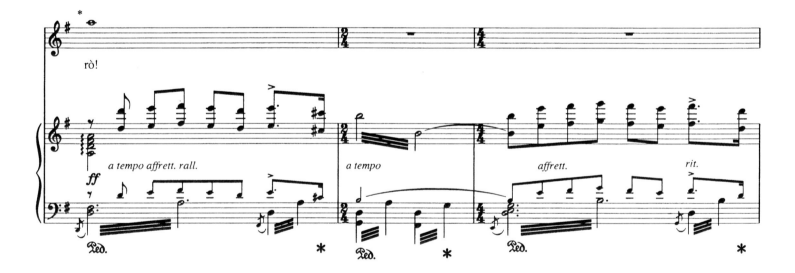

rò!

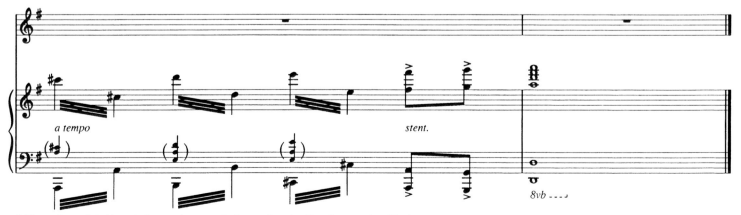

* The ending printed here is the usual one used when performing the aria as a solo with piano.